DEDICATION

To the world.

Black Cat and White Dog Search for the Meaning of Life:

A Children's Fable

BY: Kurt Broz

Illustrations By: James Neyman

Copyright © 2014 Kurt Broz

All rights reserved.

ISBN: 061570106X
ISBN-13: 978-0615701066 Kotori Books

Once upon a Saturday, there were two of the best of friends: Black Cat and White Dog. Black Cat and White Dog lived in a small apartment somewhere outside of Cleveland, in a middle-class neighborhood that sort of smelled strangely in the summer. Not bad, just strange. Sort of like a burnt Brazil nut.

White Dog was a strong and proud dog, with good pedigree and strong haunches. White Dog was tall and lean, masculine and pointy. He was born to a loving home of a cautious breeder family, and had the very best in life. White Dog spent most of his childhood eating canned dog food with fancy names, and playing with toys certified by veterinarians. White Dog was a dog of means and name, but humble to a fault. White Dog was a dog everyone loved, even those people who hate dogs. White Dog was certainly Master's favorite, and first, pet.

Black Cat hated White Dog because White Dog had it so easy. Black Cat was born in the ghetto, and found by Master in a box someone threw away in the street. Black Cat never met her parents or family, and ate off-brand dog food out of a big bag from one of those Chinese factories that probably poison you. Black Cat had a big, furry chip on her shoulder, and liked to preach about it. Unfortunately, Black Cat fell into that certain feline stereotype of being loud, lazy, and not pulling her own weight.

White Dog usually had to catch the mice because Black Cat just isn't that good at it.

KURT BROZ

BLACK CAT AND WHITE DOG SEARCH FOR THE MEANING OF LIFE: A CHILDREN'S FABLE

    Master had gone away for the weekend, and left Black Cat and White Dog with $20 for pizza. Usually, this was fine. White Dog would amuse himself by making a sporting good time of annoying the piss out of Black Cat. Whenever Black Cat would lay on the counter, tail wagging and dreaming of Fancy Feast, White Dog would make his move. He would creep up, tail tucked down tight, slowly stalking. Creeping. And then, with the fury of his wolf ancestors, he would chomp down hard on that ebony tail. Black Cat would screech and jump, clutching onto the curtains and crying. White Dog found this hilarious, and would bark triumphantly at his grandiose achievement. Good boy, thought White Dog, very good boy.

KURT BROZ

BLACK CAT AND WHITE DOG SEARCH FOR THE MEANING OF LIFE: A CHILDREN'S FABLE

Sometimes, White Dog would steal Black Cat's toys and tear them up. Sometimes, White Dog would drop bugs into Black Cat's water dish or even poop in her litter box, just because. But it was all in good fun. Every night, Black Cat and White Dog would curl up on Master's bed and sleep together. They were the best of friends despite the severe socioeconomic hurdle of their disparate backgrounds.

But this weekend, White Dog and Black Cat got an idea.

Black Cat said, "This malaise and this tedium... The ennui of life, I have had just about enough of it. Look at us; I was God in ancient Egypt, but now I just look out of a window all day. Is this all there is in the universe?"

White Dog growled, "That's some dangerous thinking, Black Cat. But, screw it, I'm pretty damned bored as well. So why don't we find out what the meaning of the life is? What this universe is all about?"

Black Cat nodded and her tail began to twitch wildly.

Black Cat meowed, "Great, but how do we do that? How do we get un-bored and find out the meaning of all of this?"

White Dog scratched his snout for a few moments and licked his crotch for a while. Black Cat sighed and thought as hard as she could, bunching up her round head and tiny nose. White Dog suddenly lit up, with hairs flapping up and out.

"Why don't we Google it? Or ask Jeeves?" wondered White Dog.

So, the two friends found Master's laptop. Neither animal had opposable thumbs, thanks to God's unflinching mercy. Luckily, however, Black Cat could type with her small, ebony paws. White Dog panted, eyes darting back and forth. Black Cat typed faster and clicked harder. After hours of searching, they had no answer.

"The internet is just a bunch of porn and zealots! There aren't any answers here!" White Dog hung his head low.

"Why don't we go outside and ask the other animals in the world? Maybe they know," Black Cat remarked. She felt awfully proud of her idea.

BLACK CAT AND WHITE DOG SEARCH FOR THE MEANING OF LIFE: A CHILDREN'S FABLE

First, Black Cat and White Dog decided to go see Butterfly. It was really out of laziness more than their belief in Butterfly's skill, as Butterfly lived in the nearby garden. Butterfly was quiet, still and sullen, not unlike a deep pool. And they always said that still waters run deep. Besides, certainly a creature who lived an entire life in the short span of a year or so would have wonderful insights into the futility of such things.

Black Cat ran up excitedly to Butterfly. "Butterfly! Butterfly! You surely must be knowledgeable of such things as life and the universe. Didn't Dylan Thomas say something about wild men who caught and sang the sun in flight?" babbled Black Cat. White Dog agreed silently, waiting for some great truths.

Butterfly said nothing.

Black Cat grew anxious after a few moments. She paced and paced. White Dog began to pace, patting the ground for a better spot to sit. After a few more moments, Butterfly sat very still, slowly moving his or her wings up and down, cleaning his or her antennae. White Dog grew restless after a few more minutes.

"Well," said White Dog, "do you have any answers at all? Any great bits of knowledge to impart on us of your existence?"

Butterfly said nothing. Butterfly fluttered off with a slight breeze.

"Fantastic," said Black Cat. "A mute or an idiot?"

BLACK CAT AND WHITE DOG SEARCH FOR THE MEANING OF LIFE: A CHILDREN'S FABLE

White Dog and Black Cat were undaunted by the task at hand. Now they had more grit and determination, thanks to the lack of response from Butterfly. Surely some creature would have the truth of truths. They wondered on, White Dog constantly barking and chasing after squirrels. Black Cat suddenly noticed a group of amphibians surrounding a toadstool near a pond. Both animal adventurers met eyes and galloped along. Was this a sermon on a mound?

As they got closer, they heard the eloquent words of Frog. Frog spoke with a throaty drawl and a slight southern accent. Frog was dark green and tinged with algae from years of living in a pond. Frog had cuts and bruises from near misses with Snake and frog-ing kids. Surely Frog had insights into the duality of animal-kind.

Frog clucked his chin and croaked as he spoke. "My friends," Frog chirped. "Gather round ye all, for I know the word and the letters of His great answers." Frog began to pace on a broken mushroom and point upward. The toads and salamanders were smitten.

Frog continued, "As Paul said to the Corinthians, be ye not of one land or one sea. Walk ye all, moist amphibians of the earth, on both land and sea, for ye shall walk My path." Frog swung his tiny arms wildly out and croaked. One of the toads stood up to shout in tongues, or so Black Cat and White Dog thought. He was really just making weird noses to catch flies. Frog rambled on and on for what seemed like hours about God and His chosen people, the amphibians.

"You may bring us disease and toxins from the people. You may bring us snakes and big fish and bullfrogs to fear. But we fear not...for You walk with us in the valley of the shadow of the reeds!" Frog got louder and louder and, in doing so, his southern accent grew heavier.

Several salamanders shouted, "Hallelujah!"

Black Cat stood up and swayed with the speech. "Frog, sir, if I may..."

"You may, child, you may," Frog said as he crunched on a grasshopper.

Black Cat spoke softly, "What is the meaning of it all? Life? The universe? Why are we here?"

Frog stroked his chin and smacked his lanky knee. He walked around thinking, of course. "Well, Black Cat, I think the answer to all your troubles is in this book." Frog thrust up the holy book of the swamp and thumbed through some pages.

White Dog, being unable to deal with the nonsense about amphibians being the chosen people and how Jesus was clearly a basilisk lizard any longer, grabbed the book away from Frog and began to read in random spots. Although the amphibians were all upset, and several female tadpoles fainted, no one was big enough to stop a dog. White Dog stopped after a few moments, handing the book to Black Cat. He turned around and began to slink off.

Frog spoke up first, "Son, what do you think the answer is now?"

White Dog paused and then said, smugly, "That I shall be an agnostic from now on, for the god of Abraham the Toad is insane. It rained people onto the Israelites? He smote the first hatches? No gay marriage despite all the homosexual animals? C'mon. I hump pillows. How is that a sin? It's all kind of silly."

Black Cat agreed. Frog was upset. He and his congregation agreed to protest outside of any animal shelters that performed dog litter abortions next weekend.

BLACK CAT AND WHITE DOG SEARCH FOR THE MEANING OF LIFE: A CHILDREN'S FABLE

Black Cat and White Dog were dejected. Butterfly and Frog didn't have any answers. Or at least any good ones. Neither really knew where to turn next, but then they stumbled on Mouse. Mouse had lived in their home for some time, but Black Cat, being both lazy and passive aggressive, commented daily to Mouse how glad she was that he helped himself to all the good food morsels. Eventually, Mouse was sick of Black Cat's attitude, and moved back outside under a big oak tree. There, he had raised 43 baby mice with his wife in the last few seasons. Raising baby mice was hard work.

Black Cat smiled a Cheshire smile. She walked up to Mouse. "Mouse, old and dear friend. We would like to...have a word with you." She purred as she spoke and rubbed against the tree. White Dog looked up from licking his privates.

"Mouse!" he exclaimed.

Mouse gulped and slinked back. Mouse was always afraid of cats and dogs and global nuclear war. Sometimes Mouse was afraid of minorities and rain, too. Mouse was afraid of a lot of things. After some explanation of their quest, Mouse agreed to help.

"We shall go see Old Mouse. Old Mouse is by far the oldest mouse in the colony. You can tell by the name, because mice don't mess around with such epitaphs. Old Mouse is old," Mouse said, matter-of-factly. White Dog and Black Cat agreed to go. They walked for a few tree blocks to a half-dead, bent pine. Most of the needles had shed on the north side and weird, red tint stained the bark.

Old Mouse creaked and stammered out of the pine tree. Old Mouse squinted and looked around. Mouse explained to Old Mouse the questions, and Old Mouse shook her head. She cleaned her classes, clockwise, and coughed.

"Ah, yes," tweeted Old Mouse. "Ah, yes. It is simple. Life is work, work is life. Here in the mouse colony, we work hard. Each has a chore and a spot. Mouse gathers seeds, Tall Mouse gathers berries, Short Mouse is a doctor, Smart Mouse is a hole digger...everyone has a place, and that place is work. When you work for the greater good, you are finding happiness and the universe."

Black Cat and White Dog were already bored of all of this. Neither particularly liked work, although far fewer cats work than dogs. And some dogs excel at work. But White Dog was not one of them. He was not a sheep herder or a police officer. Old Mouse handed White Dog and Black Cat a book. They read the cover and looked around and made a startling realization: The mice were communists, and a little bit crazy. Hipster Mouse was wearing a Che Mouseverra shirt. Old Mouse was the leader of the party.

White Dog shook his head and walked off. Black Cat shrugged her shoulders and considered her options. White Dog ran off faster, treeing a squirrel.

BLACK CAT AND WHITE DOG SEARCH FOR THE MEANING OF LIFE: A CHILDREN'S FABLE

After some time chasing squirrels, White Dog saw a weird object in a maple near a house. Black Cat was licking her dark paws in the sun. The heat rose and fell over the horizon, like a tide.

"What about Owl? He has lots of books," said White Dog. "Folks with lots of books usually know a lot of things. Maybe he has some answers. I see him up in that tree wearing those thick black glasses and drinking a coffee."

Black Cat got annoyed. "No, no," she said. "He has a lot of books but not a lot of smarts. Owl just likes to have books to appear smarter when the other birds fly over. If you actually ask him about his books, he will just walk over to one, open it, light a pipe and peer off into the distance. Then Owl strokes his feathers a bit, taps his pipe in recollection, and asks you what you think about the book. If I asked Owl his thoughts, why should I just tell him mine first?"

White Dog agreed heartily. Owl did seem smart at first, but now that White Dog thought about it, Owl was just a douche. White Dog didn't ever think he heard Owl say anything that wasn't just a quote from Melville or Morrisey.

BLACK CAT AND WHITE DOG SEARCH FOR THE MEANING OF LIFE: A CHILDREN'S FABLE

Snake was cold and calculating, but all the other animals agreed Snake was actually smart, unlike Owl or Frog. Snake was that special kind of well-read, where Snake never bothered to tell you how much he read, but he was always reading. See, Snake only had to eat maybe once or twice a month and, as he spent the rest of that month digesting one of the communist mice or religious amphibians, he could read. A lot. Snake read everything from eastern philosophy to manuals for TV's. Snake had a lot of free time on his tail. All winter long, Snake hibernated in a den with other snakes and they were a bore, so Snake read more and more. Snake often quipped that a book a day keeps the quiet grip of insanity away.

Snake was sometimes hard to find, but was usually on a big, warm rock, or sneaking into sandy play boxes to scare kids. Snake thought this was good fun and White Dog, a fan of pranks, would often help out. Everyone lets White Dog into their backyard for a good pet.

"Snake, old buddy," said White Dog. "You read. You know a lot. You get the workings of this crazy place. We have some questions on who we are, where we're going..."

Snake put up his tail to shush White Dog. Black Cat hissed. Snake flicked his tongue into the air a few times. Snake's black and brown stripes shimmered in the sun.

"White Dog," Snake slithered. "I see a lot, you see, but have no eyelids. I hear a lot, you see, but have no external ears. I read and I eat. I don't usually impose my philosophy on others, however..."

White Dog and Black Cat motioned for Snake to continue. Snake shimmied and creeped in a circle. Snake picked a tick off his back and looked around. Snake shrugged.

"You know," quipped Snake. "Because I'm, you know, a snake, no one ever fucking talks to me. I don't have any answers for you. Sure, I read. I read Nietzsche. I know Darwin and Hemingway. But, I'm still a damned snake. Because some dicks put me being evil into their version of the Bible, now even the turtles don't talk to me. Other snakes don't even like each other..."

White Dog frowned and Black Cat threw her paws up. They were both really frustrated now.

"You ever see your kids get run over by a truck? I fucking did," Snake groaned. "And another thing, some redneck chopped my mom's head off with a shovel. A shovel! I'm a damned ribbon snake. I can't kill anything but mice and goldfish. You want answers? Read the damned books yourselves."

Snake threw some books. Karl Jung hit Black Cat in the snout. White Dog gave up and scampered off to chase another squirrel. Black Cat hissed and clawed at Snake, but Snake was gone. Snake slithered off into some tall grass to feel sorry for himself some more. Snake would later turn up, drunk and medicated, eating Mouse. But that's another story for another day.

Black Cat and White Dog had almost given up. After Snake, they tried Robin and Raccoon. Robin, a pacifist, just babbled on and on about duties to other people. Neither Black Cat nor White Dog really wanted to help anyone, they just wanted answers. Raccoon was exceedingly smart but exceedingly bad. Raccoon had many answers, but was too busy breaking into garbage cans and drinking the remnants of beer cans to be bothered with great truths. Raccoon was more than happy to do bad and Raccoon explained, in detail, what a psychopath was. Raccoon was okay with this, she said, because she was also a nihilist. Neither Black Car nor White Dog cared what that was, but it sounded exhausting. Raccoon did give them both some tasty fish pieces found behind a restaurant, and they shared a smelly snack on some steps.

Eventually, Raccoon knifed a child and took his animal crackers. At that point, both Black Cat and White Dog figured it would be better to head back home than to catch some heat for that.

BLACK CAT AND WHITE DOG SEARCH FOR THE MEANING OF LIFE: A CHILDREN'S FABLE

It was getting very late and some of the stranger animals were out and about. Black Cat remembered that Bat was always out late at night, and was always high. She reasoned to White Dog that people who were high a lot had a lot of insights into things, even if they didn't make much sense and you didn't care. One time, she said, Bat had surmised just how Hershey was connected to the death of Jimmy Hoffa and it sounded really, really convincing.

White Dog found Bat flying around one of his favorite poles to pee on. Bat was hot on the heels of some moths, swooping and chirping, spiraling out of control. After a few barrel roles, Bat caught a big, juicy moth. The wings split off with the first huge bite. Bat flew down to see just what these house pets were doing out this late at night. Bat's eyes were bloodshot, and he reeked of patchouli. Bat looked slightly askew, and had some Cheeto dust on his wings.

Black Cat spoke up, "Bat, we have had quite a day and, long story short, what is the meaning of life?"

"Whoa," said Bat. Bat stepped back and put one wing on the pole. Bat lit up a rolled joint. Bat offered a hit to both Black Cat and White Dog, but they declined. Bat always had strong stuff. "I think, well, I think I know...," Bat muttered. "Like, the meaning of life... I don't think there's one meaning. I think it's whatever you want it to be. Quantum theory seems to say that there are multiple universes, parallel realities, so why should there be one answer to everything? Maybe at any one point in time, like, there are multiple answers to the question. And maybe," Bat puffed, "there's no answer and all the answers at the same time. That's...," Bat flicked a beetle off his big ear, "that's my answer to your question. Wait, what?"

Bat spun around. Someone said something somewhere, and somehow Bat's big ears picked it up. Bat looked a little nervous and maybe paranoid. White Dog shrugged. Black Cat seemed really intrigued at the answer. Black Cat looked over at White Dog, who had just treed a squirrel. He growled and jumped, falling down on his butt. Black Cat turned back but Bat had flown off after a lightning bug.

BLACK CAT AND WHITE DOG SEARCH FOR THE MEANING OF LIFE: A CHILDREN'S FABLE

Snail had only one answer, to try reading the Qur'an. That was always Snail's answer. It didn't sit well with White Dog. Tabby Cat was racist, so Black Cat refused to ask her. And all three Spiders just went on and on about the natural order of things. The Spiders always just talked about killing the weak to feed the strong and being a Republican. It was very late at night, and no one had a single valid explanation for anything in this entire universe.

White Dog and Black Cat went inside and had pretty much given up on their quest. Black Cat laughed, reminiscing about how Raccoon stole the grapes that Fox was trying to jump for. White Dog thought this was very, very funny as he dragged his butt across the floor. Black Cat licked her paws and stopped for a moment, looking into her water dish.

"I think," said Black Cat, "Bat may be right in a strange way. We make our own version of reality and our own answers." She batted some yarn and rubbed herself against the couch. "Yes, I think that's the answer. What do you say, White Dog?"

White Dog got very stoic. He stopped panting for just a few seconds and pushed his bone around in a semi-circle. He breathed in heavily and squinted in the dark.

"I know," said White Dog, "there is no point. There is nothing before or after this. We just are. I'm a dog. You are a cat. Frog is a frog. Snake is a jerk. And when I'm dead, Master will bury me in a shallow grave. No great answers, that's my belief. No point to this but just to exist for a brief, shining moment."

Black Cat's eyes grew wide and vivid green. She was startled by White Dog's sudden, stoic seriousness. Black Cat much preferred the White Dog who chased squirrels and barked at sounds he didn't understand.

"I don't like that," said Black Cat. "It may be true. It's likely true. But it makes me sad, so I choose to ignore it and insert my happier philosophy."

Just then, Black Cat saw a shape move in the corner. White Dog ran over and growled. It was just Cockroach, picking up scraps. Neither Black Cat nor White Dog liked Cockroach or his friends. They were illegal immigrants in this country, and did only gross work that even the ants wouldn't do, like eating postage stamps and crawling into people's ears at night.

BLACK CAT AND WHITE DOG SEARCH FOR THE MEANING OF LIFE: A CHILDREN'S FABLE

Cockroach froze and dropped his crumbs. Black Cat hissed and moved closer. White Dog jumped up and down, pacing back and forth, trying to show everyone his great find. Cockroach quivered and shook. Cockroach put four arms up in terror.

"You let me go, no? You let me go," Cockroach said, voice breaking in fright, "and I will let you know a secret of my people. We have seen many people and dined with kings and paupers. We have your answer."

"Humor us," spat Black Cat. White Dog wagged his tail faster and faster.

Cockroach shook and handed Black Cat and White Dog pamphlets. Cockroach nodded and said that they should look inside. All the answers would be in there, Cockroach said. As Black Cat and White Dog looked over the pamphlets, Cockroach scurried off.

"Cockroachtology? By L. Roach Hubbard? This could be..." Black Cat paused, "Interesting."

"Everyone is fucking nuts," barked White Dog. White Dog thrust his pointy nose at Black Cat. "Every--" White Dog slobbered, "--one."

Black Cat shrugged her shoulders and went back to grooming. She read her pamphlet long into the night. White Dog, having given up on his own existence that day, slept on the floor and twitched a few times during all the squirrel-chasing dreams.

ABOUT THE AUTHOR

At approximately 1:37 AM on May 27, 1983 a silent whisper broke over the land. And then there was Kurt Broz. History will surely place him amongst Caesar, Socrates, Ramses, and men of their ilk. Kurt fancies himself a writer of subterfuge concealing a cry of a humanity oppressed, desperate for a greater purpose. Kurt will be like Che Guevara for his generation... But actually successful in his thought revolution. Or maybe he's just the only one who gets the Universe's joke.

Kurt Broz is a Staff Writer for Kotori Magazine. This is his first book.

www.ingramcontent.com/pod-product-compliance
Lightning Source LLC
Chambersburg PA
CBHW041227040426
42444CB00002B/82